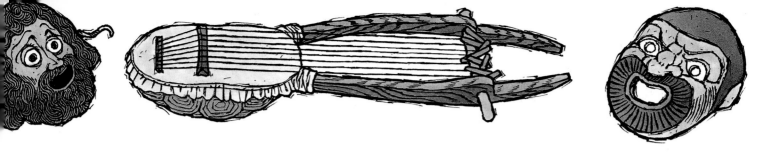

FLASHBACK HISTORY

GREEKS

Liz Gogerly

PowerKiDS
press.

New York

Published in 2010 by The Rosen Publishing Group Inc.
29 East 21st Street, New York, NY 10010

Copyright © 2010 Wayland/
The Rosen Publishing Group, Inc.

First Edition

Library of Congress Cataloging-in-Publication Data

Gogerly, Liz.
  Greeks / Liz Gogerly.
     p. cm. — (Flashback history)
  Includes index.
  ISBN 978-1-4358-5495-6 (library binding)
  ISBN 978-1-4358-5496-3 (paperback)
  ISBN 978-1-4358-5497-0 (6-pack)
  1. Greece—Civilization—To 146 B.C.—Juvenile literature. I. Title.
  DF77.G583 2010
  938—dc22
                          2009002627

Picture Acknowledgements: The Ancient Art & Architecture Collection: p16 (b), p17 (t),
p25 (b), p30 (both), p31, p39, p43 (tr); Archiv Fur Kunst und Geschichte Berlin/Eric Lessing:
p13 (b), p16 (t); Corbis cover; Courtesy The Ashmolean Museum: p21 (b); The Trustees of the
British Museum: endpapers, p8 (t), p12, p15 (t), p17 (both), p19 (both), p20. p21 (t), p23,
p33(1), p41; C.M.Dixon: p13 (t), p22 (both), p36-7; Werner Forman Archive: p24 (b);
Michael Holdford: cover, p8 (b), p9, p14, p24 (t), p25 (t), p26 (both), p27 (all), p28 (both),
p29 (t), p32, p33 (r), p34 (both), p35 (both), p37 (tl and tr), p38, p40, p42, p43 (tl), p43 (b);
Courtesy The National Tourist Organisation of Greece: p29 (b); Courtesy Wurzbury Museum:
p15 (b).

Every effort has been made to clear copyright. Should there be any inadvertent omission, please
apply to the publisher for rectification.

Endpapers: Young horsemen and boys in the procession in honor of the goddess Athena.
This is from the Parthenon frieze in Athens and dates from the fifth century BCE.

Manufactured in China

Maple Press 1/14/10 $ 19.95

CONTENTS

Words that appear in **bold** can be found in the glossary on page 44.

WHO WERE THE GREEKS?

Ancient Greece was never one united country like it is today. Instead, it was made up of hundreds of city-states such as Athens, Corinth, and Sparta (see map on page 9). Each city-state had its own main city, government, and army.

THE ACROPOLIS ▼

Athens was the strongest **city-state**. Many weaker states paid the Athenians to defend them if they were attacked by other city-states. Athens became rich as well as great. Much of its wealth was spent on the fine temples on the **Acropolis** (see below).

LIFE IN ATHENS ▶

Athens reached the height of its power in the fifth century BCE. The city became a famous center of art, culture, learning, and politics. Pottery from this time was often decorated with scenes from everyday life. The vase on the right shows rich Athenians relaxing and enjoying music.

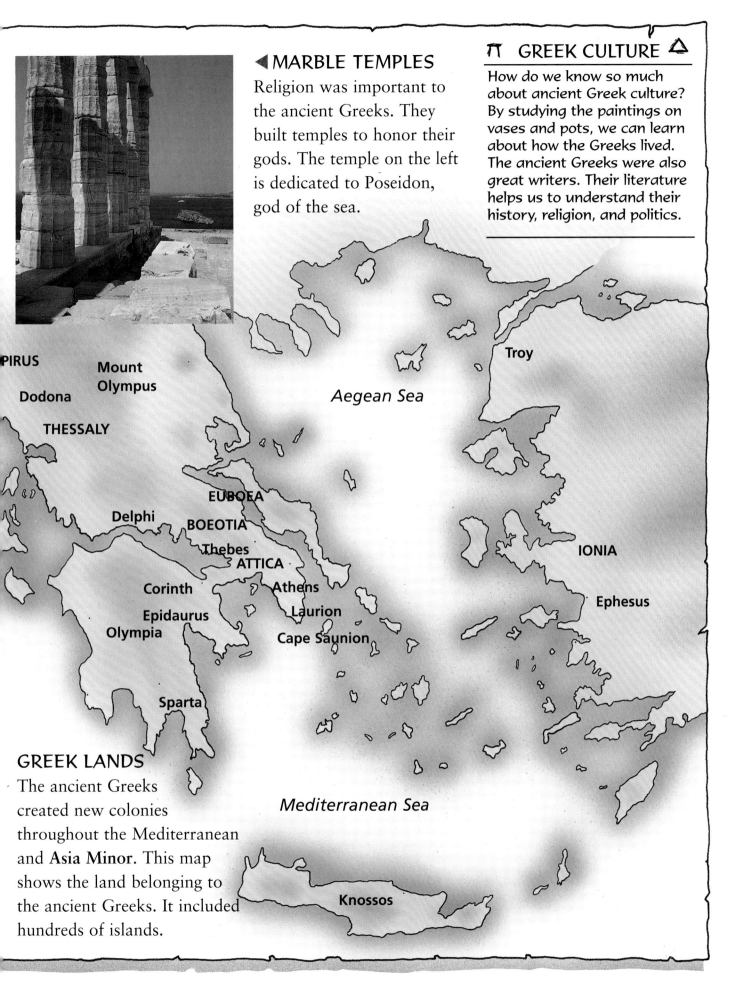

◀ MARBLE TEMPLES

Religion was important to the ancient Greeks. They built temples to honor their gods. The temple on the left is dedicated to Poseidon, god of the sea.

𝝅 GREEK CULTURE △

How do we know so much about ancient Greek culture? By studying the paintings on vases and pots, we can learn about how the Greeks lived. The ancient Greeks were also great writers. Their literature helps us to understand their history, religion, and politics.

PIRUS

Mount Olympus

Dodona

THESSALY

Aegean Sea

Troy

Delphi

EUBOEA

BOEOTIA

Thebes

ATTICA

Corinth

Athens

Epidaurus

Laurion

Olympia

Cape Saunion

IONIA

Ephesus

Sparta

GREEK LANDS

The ancient Greeks created new colonies throughout the Mediterranean and **Asia Minor**. This map shows the land belonging to the ancient Greeks. It included hundreds of islands.

Mediterranean Sea

Knossos

9

TIMELINE

	2000 BCE	1800 BCE	1500 BCE	1200 BCE	1000 BCE
EVENTS IN GREECE	Arrival of the first Greek-speaking people on mainland Greece.	Rise of the Mycenaean civilization in Greece.	Fall of the Minoans. Fall of the Mycenaeans.	Phoenicians spread throughout the Mediterranean. Some Greeks colonize Asia Minor. Beginning of the Trojan War.	Iron is first introduced to Greece.
PERIOD IN WESTERN HISTORY	Bronze Age ca. 2900–1000 BCE				Dark Age ca.1100–800 BCE
EVENTS IN BRITAIN	Stonehenge is built in Britain.				
EVENTS AROUND THE WORLD	Rise of the Indus Valley civilizations in Pakistan. Rise of Babylon.		Reign of the Egyptian New Kingdom. Hittite Empire reaches its height in Asia.		

Minoan script disk

Mycenaean pot

Egyptian head

800 BCE	600 BCE	500 BCE	400 BCE	200 BCE
Greek alphabet is invented. 776 BCE First Olympic Games. ca. 750 BCE Homer believed to have lived. Greeks found colonies in Ionia and Black Sea.	Coins are introduced in Greece. Sparta takes control of the Peloponnese peninsula. Democracy begins in Athens	546 BCE Persian invasion of Greece begins. 534 BCE The first Greek tragedy is performed. Athens at its most powerful.	ca. 448–432 BCE Parthenon is built in Athens. 431–404 BCE Peloponnesian Wars between Athens and Sparta. 336 BCE Alexander the Great is ruler of Greece.	ca. 275–146 BCE The Romans conquer the Greek Empire.
Archaic Period ca. 800–500 BCE **Homer**		Classical Period ca. 500–323 BCE	**Alexander the Great** / Hellenistic Period ca. 323–30 BCE	
	Celtic people arrive in southeast England.	**The Parthenon**	Roman armies invade Britain.	
Rise of Etruscan civilization in Italy. 735 BCE City of Rome is founded. Reign of the Chou dynasty in China.	The Assyrians conquer Lower Egypt. Rise of the Persian Empire.	First copper is used in Africa.	Maya civilization rises in Central America.	Egypt becomes part of the Roman Empire 221 BCE The Great Wall of China is built.

THE LEGEND OF TROY

The Greek poet Homer lived in the Dark Age. We know something about that time from his famous works, *The Iliad* and *The Odyssey*. In *The Iliad*, Homer wrote about how the Greeks managed to invade the city of Troy in **Asia Minor**. Greek soldiers hid inside a huge wooden horse. The Trojans were interested in the horse, so they dragged it inside their city. That night, the Greeks crept out of the horse and captured Troy.

PERIODS OF GREEK HISTORY

circa 2900–1000 BCE
The Bronze Age

circa 1100–800 BCE
The Dark Age

circa 800–500 BCE
The Archaic Period

circa 500–323 BCE
The Classical Period

circa 323–30 BCE
The Hellenistic Period

WHERE DID THE GREEKS GET THEIR FOOD?

Farmers worked hard in the hot climate to raise crops. Olives and grapes were the most important crops. They grew green vegetables and beans. Fruits included pears, pomegranates, and apples. Barley and wheat were grown to make bread. Farmers used sharp sickles (see below) to cut the grain.

◀ OLIVE GROVES

Today, Greece is famous for its olives. It was the same in ancient times. Olive trees do well in the dry rocky soil of Greece. This vase painting (see left) shows the olives being harvested. The fruit is eaten whole or crushed to make olive oil. In the past, the oil was used for everything from cooking to washing the skin.

FARM ANIMALS

Greece is very dry so there were not many fields for animals. Goats were the most common farm animals, because they do well in dry areas. They provided milk and cheese. Some farmers managed to raise pigs and poultry. Meat from these animals was a luxury. Oxen, mules, and donkeys were used to pull plows and carts.

Sickle

HUNTING

Below you can see a huntsman with his dog. In his catch, he has a fox and a hare. The ancient Greeks also hunted wild boar and deer. Birds such as swans, geese, thrushes, and nightingales were regularly caught, too.

Bill hook

Pickax

 ## FOOD AND THE GODS

Some foods became linked to particular Greek gods. The goddess Athena was believed to have made the first olive tree grow in Athens. Dionysos was the god of wine and barley. Many cups and jugs used for storing wine were decorated with pictures of him. Demeter was the goddess of agriculture.

◀ FISHING

The seas around ancient Greece were filled with seafood. Tuna, mackerel, squid, octopus, and shellfish were common. The fishermen on this vase have caught fish using simple rods.

DID THE GREEKS EAT WELL?

People in ancient Greece had a healthy, balanced diet. Breakfast and lunch were light meals. They usually ate bread with figs, olives, and cheese. The main meal was eaten in the evening. Most people ate fish with vegetables.

◀ A DRINKING PARTY

This vase (left) shows men at a drinking party (*symposium*). They lay on couches and were served food and drinks by slaves. Sometimes they played games or listened to music.

Cabbage

Lettuce

PARTY FOOD ▶

Many different courses were served at the *symposium*. The feast began with little dishes of jellyfish, pine nuts, celery, dates, and oysters. The main course was usually fish flavored with herbs such as oregano and bay. There were side dishes of vine leaves and fennel. Afterward, there were nuts, figs, grapes, cheeses, and delicious cakes sweetened with fruit and honey.

Bread

Figs

Dates

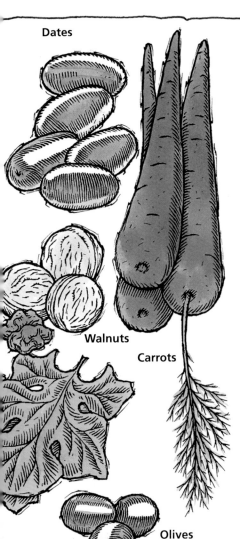

Walnuts

Carrots

Olives

Parsnips

Grapes

FISH DISH ▶

Archaeologists have found many plates decorated with fish (see right). These plates often have a hollow in the middle. This was probably filled with a sauce to go with the fish.

CUPS, JUGS, AND BOWLS

Most of the pots you see in museums today were used as containers for food.

The Greeks always mixed their wine with water in a big mixing bowl called a krater. Jugs, called oinochoe, were dipped into the krater to fill the large drinking cups. A hydria, or water pot, has three handles. The amphora, for wine or oil, has two.

SLAVE GIRLS ▶

Only men were invited to drinking parties. However, slave girls served the wine and danced for the guests. The vase on the right shows a girl helping a sick guest. He's probably drunk too much wine!

DID THE GREEKS HAVE FAMILIES LIKE OURS?

We know a lot about family life in Athens from ancient Greek writers. They wrote about a civilization where men were the head of the family. Families usually had more children than they do now.

MARRIAGE AND CHILDBIRTH ▼

Many women died while giving birth. Below you can see a carved stone made for the grave of a young mother. Many carvings like this have been found. They usually show the mother with her child.

WOMEN AT HOME ▲

In ancient Greece, a woman's place was in the home. In Athens, rich women had an escort when they went out. Mostly, women stayed indoors and rarely saw their husbands. Many girls were married when they reached 13. Women were responsible for running the household. They looked after the children and organized the slaves. The vase painting above shows a young woman at work weaving and spinning wool.

DOLLS ▶

Like today, ancient Greek children enjoyed playing with dolls. **Archaeologists** have found many clay dolls like the one you can see on the right. The arms and legs are joined together so they can move. Originally, this doll would have had a painted face and clothes.

SPECIAL DAYS IN CHILDHOOD

At ten days old, a baby was named and the family celebrated their birth. At 12 or 13 years old, a special ceremony for the child was held at the temple. Each child took their toys to the temple and dedicated them to the gods. This was a symbol that they were leaving childhood behind. Soon after this, the girls would get married.

Here is a dedication to the goddess Artemis:

"Maiden goddess, to you before her marriage, Timarete gives
Her cap, her tambourine, her favorite ball,
And as is proper, O Artemis,
Her childhood toys, her dolls, her all."

GAMES AND TOYS ▼

The ancient Greeks enjoyed playing with games and toys. Babies had clay rattles that were modeled into animals like pigs or owls (see below). Younger children had carts to pull around on pieces of string. Older children used hoops and sticks, balls and spinning tops. Adults and children played board games similar to checkers. All of these toys and games were homemade using clay, wood, and animal bones.

▲ LOVE AND WAR

War was a fact of life in ancient Greece. Fighting between **city-states** was common, and the men were often called away to fight. The drinking cup above shows a girl saying farewell to her husband. As she fills his cup with wine, she knows she might never see him again.

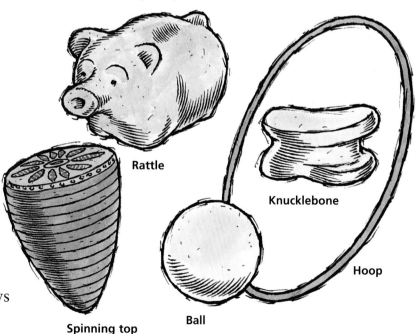

Rattle

Knucklebone

Hoop

Ball

Spinning top

DID THE GREEKS LIVE IN HOUSES?

Many ancient Greek temples still stand today. These were built of solid stone or marble, and have survived over thousands of years. Ordinary Greek houses were built of mud bricks so they have mostly crumbled away. Archaeologists have discovered the remains of some small homes. These ruins give us many clues about how the Greeks made their houses.

Kitchen

Courtyard

Bedroom

Andron

Main door

A GREEK HOUSE ▲

Above is the plan of a typical Greek house. The size of the house depended on how rich the family was, but the layout was always similar. The rooms of the house were arranged around a courtyard. Most families placed an altar in the courtyard.

In those days, men and women had separate rooms. Women had their own quarters called the *gynaeceum*, where they worked and ate. Men had a room called the *andron*. Im was here where they held their *symposium* (see page 14).

A NEW HOME ▼

On the vase below you can see a bride entering her new home. Sweets and nuts were showered over her and her husband as a symbol of happiness and prosperity.

COMFY COUCHES ▶

The vase on the right shows a man on a couch. It looks very much like a bed. It was made of wood and covered with a mattress and cushions.

Beside the couch, youcan see a low rectangular table. It would have had three legs rather than four. When the man finished his meal, the table would have been pushed under the couch.

 SIMPLE FURNITURE

Greek homes did not have much furniture. Usually people just had tables, chairs, stools, couches, and beds. Archaeologists have found beautiful examples of simple furniture. Tables and chairs were often made of light wood. Sometimes they were decorated with ivory, gold, and silver.

There were two kinds of chair. There was a big, high-backed chair called a thronos, which the man of the house sat on. There was also a smaller chair with curved legs called a klismos.

Pots and other possessions were usually hung on the walls. Women kept their personal possessions in baskets and small boxes.

DID BOYS AND GIRLS GO TO SCHOOL?

In Athens and other towns, there were private schools for rich boys. All girls were educated at home, but from the age of seven, boys were sent to school. At school, the boys learned reading, writing, public speaking, sports, and music.

WRITING TOOLS ▼

At first, boys wrote on wax tablets. They used a bronze tool called a *stylus* for writing. The flat end of the *stylus* was used to smooth out their mistakes. When they were older, boys wrote on a kind of paper called *papyrus*. Ink was made from soot and vegetable gum. They wrote with a reed pen.

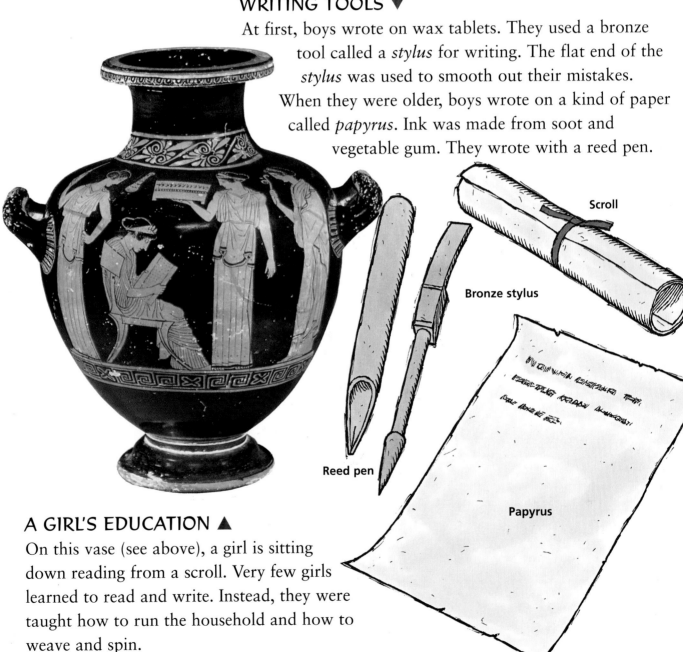

Scroll

Bronze stylus

Reed pen

Papyrus

A GIRL'S EDUCATION ▲

On this vase (see above), a girl is sitting down reading from a scroll. Very few girls learned to read and write. Instead, they were taught how to run the household and how to weave and spin.

MUSIC ▲

Music was important to the ancient Greeks, so all boys learned how to play an instrument. The most popular instruments were the *lyre* (a stringed instrument), the *kithara* (a stringed instrument that was bigger than the *lyre*), and the *aulos* (a kind of flute).

EXERCISE ▶

At 12 years old, boys began physical education so they would grow up to become fit and strong soldiers. The Greeks believed keeping fit was as important as reading and writing. On the right, you can see a drinking cup with a picture of a boy running with a hoop. A teacher called a *paidotribe* would have taught him dancing and athletics.

Θ THE ALPHABET ✎

These are the letters of the Greek alphabet.

A A	**B** B	**Γ** G	**Δ** D
E E	**Z** Z	**H** EE/AY	**Θ** TH
I I	**K** K	**Λ** L	**M** M
N N	**Ξ** X/KS	**O** O	**Π** P
P R	**Σ** S	**T** T	**Y** U/OO
Φ F/PH	**X** CH	**Ψ** PS	**Ω** OH

WHO WENT TO WORK IN GREEK TIMES?

In the countryside, most people worked as farmers. In the towns, there were many different jobs. There were shopkeepers and merchants. Craftsmen specialized in making pottery, jewelry, sculpture, cloth, and shoes. There were professional workers, such as doctors, lawyers, and teachers. Throughout Greece there were slaves.

WOMAN'S WORK ▼

Below you can see a clay model of a woman kneading dough. She was probably a slave. Household slaves were usually treated quite well by their owners.

SLAVES IN THE HOME ▲

Look at the vase above and you can see the mistress of a household with a slave girl. She is passing her a large bundle of pink cloth. Perhaps this cloth is for making clothes, or it could be laundry.

The young girl would have been a slave. Slaves and their children belonged to the master and mistress of the house.

CRAFTSMEN AT WORK ▶

Archaeologists have discovered many objects made by Greek craftsmen. Bronze was used to make all kinds of objects including sculptures, cooking utensils, jewelry, lamps, and horse harnesses. Stone and marble were used as building materials. Unfortunately, most woodwork has rotted away. On the right, you can see a carpenter at work.

MAKING CLOTH ▼

Women spent much of their time at home where they organized the production of cloth. First of all, the wool was washed and dyed. Then it was spun into yarn using a **distaff** and **spindle**. Finally, the yarn was woven into cloth on a loom.

Spindle

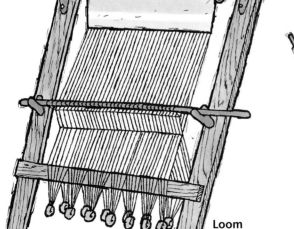
Loom

Distaff

SLAVES

By the fifth century BCE, there were about 100,000 slaves in the region around Athens called Attica. This was twice the number of free citizens. Many slaves were kidnapped and captured during war. Slaves were born into slavery, if their parents were slaves. Slaves had no legal rights and had to do exactly as they were told.

WHAT DID THE GREEKS DO IN THEIR SPARE TIME?

Festivals in honor of the gods took place throughout the year. Festivals for Dionysos, the god of wine, were celebrated with the drinking of wine, dancing, and singing. The Olympic Games were held in honor of Zeus, king of all gods. People also celebrated harvest time, weddings, and birthdays.

◀ **FESTIVAL GAMES**

A grand festival in honor of the goddess Athena was held in Athens every four years, Part of the celebrations was the famous games. People competed in different athletic events. The winner of each event was awarded a vase called a Panathenaic *amphora*. The vase on the left was given to the winner of the horse-racing competition.

KNUCKLEBONES ▶

On the right, you can see two women playing the popular Greek game of knucklebones, a game of luck played using the bones of small animals. Each player threw their knucklebones into the air and attempted to catch them all on the back of one hand.

◀ LONG JUMP

One of the most exciting competitions at any games was the **pentathlon** ("five events"). The long jump was one of the five events. This vase shows that the athlete is holding a pair of jumping weights. These were swung behind him to help him jump farther.

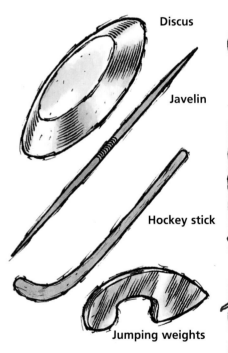

Discus

Javelin

Hockey stick

Jumping weights

FAVORITE GAMES

Popular events at the games included:

- Running • Horse-racing • Chariot-racing
- Boxing • Wrestling • Throwing the Discus
- Long Jump • Throwing the Javelin

One of the most dangerous sports was the pankration. It was a cross between boxing and wrestling.

◀ CRUEL SPORTS

The Greeks liked to think of themselves as civilized people, and cruelty to animals was not popular. Sometimes the Greeks did amuse themselves with cruel sports, though. This carved **relief** shows spectators enjoying a fight between a dog and a cat.

WHAT DID THE GREEKS WEAR?

Men, women, and children were dressed in similar clothes. People mostly wore tunics and cloaks. Clothes were usually made from finely spun wool or linen. These fabrics helped to keep them cool in the hot climate. The Greeks also liked bright colors. Footwear included leather sandals and boots.

FASHIONABLE WOMEN ▼

Below, you can see two fashionable Greek ladies. They are both wearing a tunic called a *chiton*. On top, they are wearing a cloak called a *himation*. It was traditional for married women to wear the *himation* pulled up to cover the head like the woman on the right.

JEWELRY ▼

Greek women enjoyed wearing necklaces, bracelets, earrings, diadems, and anklets. These were often made of gold, silver, amber, jade, or ivory. Sometimes they were decorated with gems.

WEDDING DAY ▶

On the right, you can see a bride being dressed for her wedding. She is probably wearing a silk *peplos*. In those days silk was a luxury that only the rich could afford.

▼ MEN'S CLOTHES

Men usually wore a tunic. Sometimes they wore the tunic wrapped around the body and thrown over the shoulder (see the man below on the left). This was called the *exomis*. A tunic worn over both shoulders was called the *chiton*. Little clay balls were often used to weigh down the tunic. This helped it to fall in perfect folds.

TUNIC STYLES

Like today, the Greeks had changing fashions. The earliest tunic was the Doric peplos.

This tunic was worn by women. It was fastened at the shoulder with a long pin, and there was an overfold of fabric at the top.

Doric *peplos*

Later, there was the Ionic chiton. This was worn by men and women. It was arranged on the shoulders to form loose, elbow-length sleeves.

Ionic *chiton*

WAS RELIGION IMPORTANT IN ANCIENT GREECE?

Religion played a big part in everyday life. The Greeks worshiped many gods and goddesses. They believed that the gods controlled everything from the weather to a good harvest. By offering prayers and sacrifices, they hoped to please the gods. In return, they believed the gods would look after them.

◀ PERSEPHONE

On the left is a clay statuette of Persephone, goddess of the **Underworld**. She represents innocence and youthfulness of women. She is also linked to spring and renewed hope.

▲ ZEUS AND ATHENA

Many of the stories about the gods and goddesses are extraordinary. The vase painting above shows the birth of the goddess Athena. She was born from the head of her father Zeus. To the right stands Hephaistos, the smith god. He is holding an axe with which he has cracked open Zeus's head so that Athena could be born.

◄ HERACLES

The dramatic scene on this vase shows the hero, Heracles, fighting with a sea monster. The monster is Triton, a dangerous son of Poseidon, god of the sea. It is half-fish and half-human. It has a long, scaly, forked tail.

DELPHI ►

The most important gods were known by all Greeks and had great temples dedicated to them. In this photograph, you can see the ancient ruins at Delphi (see map page 9). At this site, you can see a famous **shrine** dedicated to the worship of Apollo. He was the god of music, light, and healing, and always appears as a beautiful young man in Greek art.

THE FAMILY OF GODS

The most important gods were thought to live on Mount Olympus. They were known as the Olympians. On the right, you can see some of the Olympians. At the top there is Zeus, the king of the gods. He is holding a thunderbolt. Below him is his wife, the goddess Hera.

Hestia, the goddess of the hearth, is sitting down. Athena (bottom, left) is the goddess of wisdom and warfare. She is holding an owl because it represents wisdom. Finally, you can see Ares, the god of war (bottom, right).

DID THE GREEKS GO TO THE DOCTOR?

The Greeks thought that sickness and disease were punishments sent by the gods. When they were sick, they prayed to Asclepios, the god of medicine and healing. There were all kinds of doctors in ancient Greece. The most famous doctor was Hippocrates.

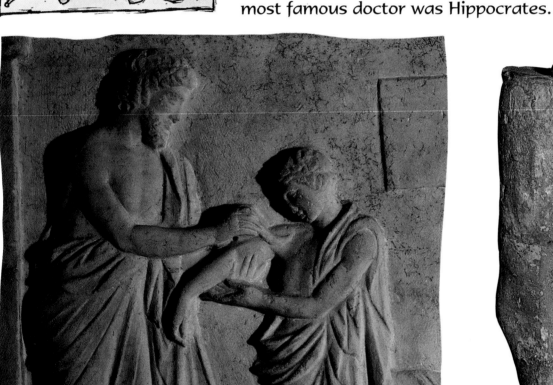

A HEALING HAND ▲

Above, you can see a doctor treating a boy. Many Greek doctors followed the methods of Hippocrates. He was the first person who tried to understand how the body worked.

OFFERINGS ▶

People made **offerings** to Asclepios. This terra-cotta model of a leg would have been offered by a person with a bad leg.

SURGICAL INSTRUMENTS ▼

The ancient Greeks practiced surgery. Below, there is a selection of surgical instruments. Many of these instruments have survived because they are made from iron or bronze. **Archaeologists** have discovered scalpels, knives, probes, and hooks.

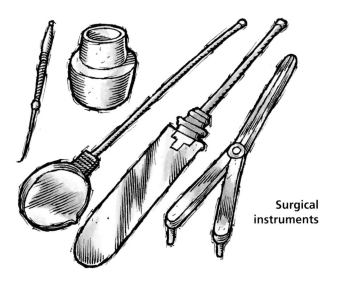

Surgical
instruments

WHAT A PAIN!

The ancient Greeks operated on different parts of the body. They even amputated limbs when they needed to. Unfortunately, they did not have the powerful anesthetics that we have today. They often used opium and a herb called mandrake instead. These did not always work properly, so operations must have been painful and dangerous.

ASCLEPIOS ▶

Even when doctors managed to cure people, the Greeks still believed in the god Asclepios. To the right is a sculpture of Asclepios. According to legend, he was the son of Apollo and was brought up by a **centaur,** who taught him the art of medicine.

WHO RULED THE GREEKS?

Greece was made up of independent city-states. In early times, each city-state was ruled by a single leader, called a tyrant. During the fifth century BCE, Athens became the first city-state to introduce democracy. *Democracy* means "rule by the people." This system allowed the citizens to vote for the leader of their choice. Women, slaves, and foreigners were not allowed to vote.

▼ ALEXANDER THE GREAT

This bronze statuette is of Alexander the Great. In 336 BCE, Alexander became King of Macedonia in the northeast of Greece. He was a very successful soldier. Through his military conquests, he built up a huge empire.

He defeated the Persians and captured territories in **Asia Minor**, Egypt, and India. These conquests were responsible for spreading Greek culture far beyond Greece.

PERICLES ▶

On the right is a bust of Pericles, the great leader and *strategos* of Athens from 443 to 429 BCE. He was a great supporter of **democracy**. He was elected leader of Athens 15 times. He was also responsible for some of Athens' buildings, including the Parthenon.

▲ DEMOCRACY IN PRACTICE

The Athenians could get rid of politicians they did not like. At the **Assembly,** people would write the name of the politician on pieces of pot (*ostrakon*), see below. In the scene above, a number of Greeks are casting their votes. If enough people voted against a person, he was exiled from Athens for 10 years.

Ostrakon

 THE ASSEMBLY

Every citizen had the right to speak at the Assembly in Athens. It met on a hill called the Pnyx. About 6,000 people gathered at the Assembly every 10 days. People also voted on matters of importance, such as how public money should be spent or whether Athens should go to war. They voted for or against a proposal with a show of hands.

WERE THE GREEKS ARTISTS?

The ancient Greeks are famous for their art. Statues and carvings of the gods and goddesses were used to decorate temples and important buildings. Everyday objects were beautifully decorated.

◀ LIFELIKE SCULPTURES

The human body was one of the most popular subjects for artists. Sculptors created lifelike figures in marble and bronze. This statue of a young man was carved in 490 BCE. He may have been a famous athlete made to resemble the god Apollo.

VASE PAINTING ▲

The Greeks were also well known for their vase painting. Artists usually used black, orange, and red clay paints. The vase above is painted in the red-figure style. It shows one of the adventures of Odysseus. This time he is tempted with the singing of the **Sirens**.

▼ POTTERY STYLES

On the left is a group of vases and pots painted in different styles. As well as painting everyday scenes, the Greeks loved to show episodes from their favorite **myths** and legends.

In the sixth century BCE, vases were painted in the black-figure style. Figures were painted in black and the background left in a reddish-brown color. By the fifth century, the red-figure style took over and the background was black, with the figures in reddish brown.

STATUE OF A GOD ▶

On the right is a fine example of a bronze head of a god. Originally, this would have been part of a statue. It would have had glass or marble eyes and bronze eyelashes! Not many Greek bronze statues have survived. Fortunately, the most famous statues were copied by Roman sculptors. You can still see these in museums today.

VASE NAMES

Dinos—Bowl for mixing wine and water

Olpe—Jug for wine

Pyxis—Cosmetic box

Aryballos—Perfume bottle

Kylix—Drinking cup

DID THE GREEKS GO TO THE THEATER?

The Greeks loved going to the theater. Plays were either tragedies or comedies. As well as main actors, there was a group of people called a chorus. The chorus danced and told the story of the play, Greek plays were shown in open-air theaters. The audience sat on seats arranged around a circular space known as the orchestra.

◄ MASKS

Actors wore masks made of stiffened linen or clay. Male and female parts were played by men. The actors changed masks to move from one part to another.

OPEN-AIR THEATER ►

This is a photograph of a theater at Dodona in northern Greece. The theater is built into a hillside. The seats rise naturally in tiers, so people can see what is happening on the stage below. This theater could have seated 14,000 people. The back wall of the stage was called the *skene*, which is where our word *scenery* comes from.

COMEDIES ▲

The Greeks certainly had a good sense of humor. The vase painting above shows a scene from a comedy. The actors are wearing big masks designed to make the audience laugh. Their clothes are padded around the stomach and bottoms to make them look funny.

SOPHOCLES ▲

The most famous authors of tragic plays were Aeschylus, Sophocles, and Euripides. Above is a Roman portrait of Sophocles, who was born about 496 BCE. He wrote *King Oedipus*, *Antigone*, and *Electra*.

📖 THEATER FACTS

- Plays were put on at festival times in Athens.

- The male citizens of Athens made up most of the audience.

- People brought their own cushions to sit on.

- Special effects included rolling pebbles on copper sheets to imitate the sound of thunder.

WERE THE GREEKS SCIENTISTS?

The Greeks' skill in science and technology is most clearly seen in their temple architecture. Temples were made of limestone or marble pillars, which had to be made and then put in place. The Greeks invented new machinery to help them with their building projects.

TEMPLE BUILDING ▼

Building a temple was a job for skilled engineers. The columns that formed a tall **colonnade** around the building were made up of massive cylinders of stone. These were held together with metal pegs. The stones were lifted into place using ropes and pulleys.

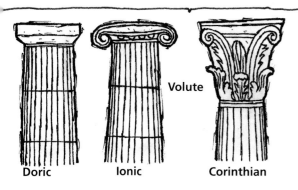

Doric   Ionic   Corinthian

Volute

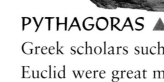

Capital

▲ ARCHITECTURAL STYLES

In Greek temples, there were three main styles (see above). The Doric column was popular in mainland Greece. The top of each column was plain. In the eastern parts of Greece and the islands, the Ionic style was more common. The columns were thinner and each top was decorated with scroll-like forms called *volutes*. The Corinthian pillar had carvings in the shape of **acanthus leaves**.

PYTHAGORAS ▲

Greek scholars such as Pythagoras and Euclid were great mathematicians. Above is a bust of Pythagoras. His theorem on triangles is still used in geometry today.

ARCHIMEDES ▼

Archimedes was a brilliant inventor and mathematician. He invented the Archimedes screw. This device was used to raise water from one level to another. He also discovered how levers and pulleys could be used to lift heavy weights.

 ASTRONOMY

The Greeks were fascinated by the stars. Astronomers made some amazing discoveries:

• Thales found out what caused an eclipse of the Sun.

• Aristarchus worked out that the Earth moved around the Sun.

• Anaxagoras realized that the Moon's light is reflected from the Sun.

• Hipparchus located 850 stars.

DID THE GREEKS GO ON LONG JOURNEYS?

Greece was a great seafaring nation. Travel by sea was the only way to reach the hundreds of islands that made up Greece. They also needed to reach Greek colonies and faraway places such as Egypt, Spain, and Africa. Large, heavy merchant ships could travel long distances.

MERCHANTS AND PIRATES ▼

Sailors usually sailed close to the shore on their voyages. This was in case of sudden storms or attacks by pirates. The vase below shows a merchant ship being taken by pirates. On the pirate ship, you can see a pointed **prow,** which was used to ram the merchant's boat.

TRAVEL OVERLAND ▶

Greece is a mountainous country, so it was difficult to make long journeys by road. Travel on land was by horse or donkey. On the right, you can see a person on a horse. In those days only rich people could afford horses.

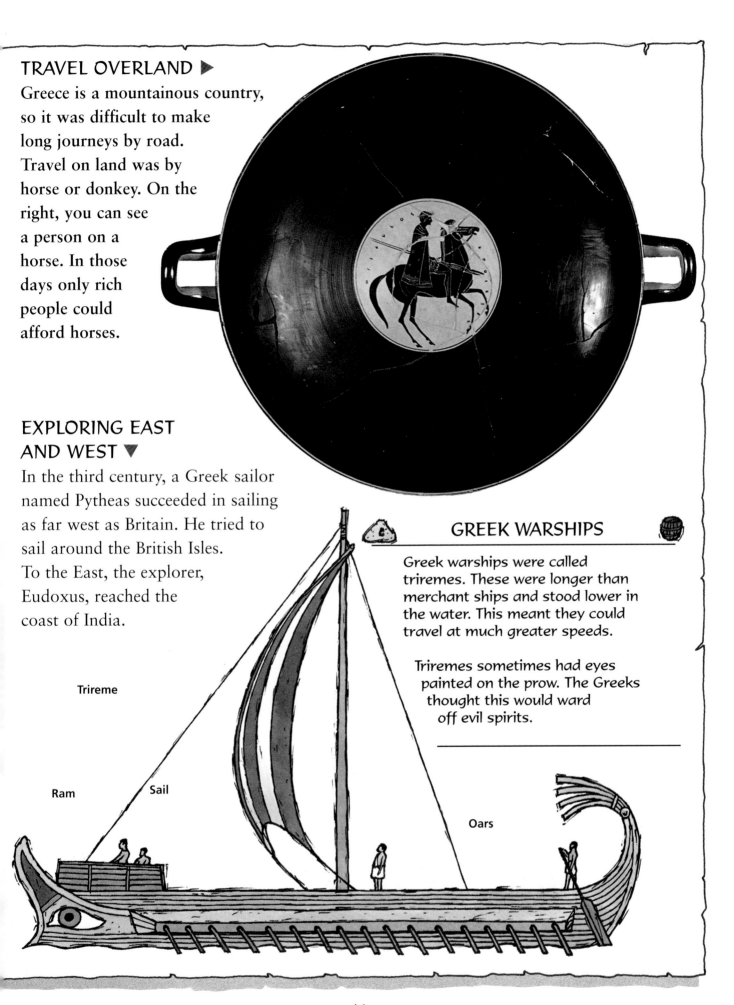

EXPLORING EAST AND WEST ▼

In the third century, a Greek sailor named Pytheas succeeded in sailing as far west as Britain. He tried to sail around the British Isles. To the East, the explorer, Eudoxus, reached the coast of India.

Trireme

Ram

Sail

Oars

GREEK WARSHIPS

Greek warships were called triremes. These were longer than merchant ships and stood lower in the water. This meant they could travel at much greater speeds.

Triremes sometimes had eyes painted on the prow. The Greeks thought this would ward off evil spirits.

WHAT WAS LIFE LIKE IN THE ARMY?

In Athens, young men of 18 did two years of military training. For the next 40 years of their life, they were supposed to keep fit and ready to fight. War was the biggest test for any Greek man. To die in battle was the greatest honor.

HELMET ▼

Greek soldiers had to pay for their own armor and weapons. This is a Greek helmet. Some helmets had horsehair crests.

GREEK SOLDIERS ▼

Greek foot soldiers were called *hoplites*. Below, you can see a hoplite wearing armor. The body armor or *cuirass* is made of bronze and leather. On his legs, he wears greaves made of leather or metal. He fought with spears and swords.

AT BATTLE ▼

Fighting was often the subject of Greek **myths**. Below is a vase showing Achilles killing an Amazon warrior queen named Penthesilea. They are fighting with spears.

SPARTAN SOLDIER ▶

This bronze figure of a Spartan soldier on the right dates from the fifth century BCE. Spartan soldiers were famous for their bravery. They spent most of their life fighting and rarely saw their families.

ARCHERS AND STONE-SLINGERS ▼

By the fourth century BCE, the Greeks used archers and stone-slingers in battle. These men could not afford armor and were used as backup troops. This cup below shows an archer from Scythia.

MILITARY SCHOOL

The city of Sparta (see map on page 9) was the great enemy of Athens. By the fifth century BCE, Sparta had become the strongest military power in Greece. The Spartans were obsessed with war. Boys lived at home with their parents until the age of seven. Then they went to live in military-style schools and trained as soldiers. They went barefoot and ate simple food. They even competed against each other to see who could stand the most flogging.

GLOSSARY, FURTHER INFORMATION, AND WEB SITES

ACANTHUS LEAVES A plant or shrub with spiny leaves.

ACROPOLIS The Greek word means "high city." It was the most defended part of a Greek city. The most famous acropolis was at Athens.

ALTAR A place, often a table, where people can lay offerings to gods and goddesses.

ANDRON Dining room in a house. It was only used by men.

ARCHAEOLOGIST A person who studies history and the past. They do this by digging up old buildings and finding objects.

ASIA MINOR An area known as Ionia in Ancient Greek times. It included most of modern Turkey.

ASSEMBLY The meeting of citizens to discuss the affairs of the city-state.

CENTAUR A creature from Greek myth. It had the body and legs of a horse, and the chest, arms, and head of a man.

CITY-STATE A city and its surrounding farmland.

COLONNADE A row of columns.

DEMOCRACY A political system that began in Greece. The word is made from two Greek words meaning "people" and "power." Basically, it means people have the right to vote on matters of government.

DIADEM A hair decoration that looks like a crown.

DISTAFF A stick holding wool. It is used when spinning wool by hand.

ESCORT A person who accompanies a woman when she goes out in public.

FLOGGING Beating with a stick or whip.

HEARTH The floor or area in front of a fireplace.

HOPLITES A Greek foot soldier. He carried a spear and protected himself with a large shield.

MYTH An old story or legend about the gods or heroes.

OFFERING Anything offered as a sacrifice or symbol of devotion to the gods. Typical offerings were fruit, vegetables, and flowers.

PENTATHLON A contest of five events: running, jumping, throwing the discus and the javelin, and wrestling.

PROW The pointed front of a ship.

RELIEF A type of carving. Parts of the design stand out from the surface.

SHRINE A holy building or place where people can place offerings to the gods.

SIRENS Homer wrote about the Sirens in *The Odyssey*. These creatures were half-women and half-bird. Their songs tempted sailors to the shoreline, where they would die on the rocks.

SPINDLE A small bar used for twisting and winding wool.

STRATEGOS An Athenian army commander. Ten were elected each year.

TRIREME A long Greek warship. It had three levels and room for 170 oarsmen. Its main weapon was an underwater ram.

UNDERWORLD The place where the ancient Greeks believed people went when they died. Sometimes known as Hades.

Books to read

Life in Ancient Greece
by Lynn Peppas (Crabtree Publishing, 2004)

Myths of the Ancient Greeks
by Richard P Martin (NAL, 2003)

People of the Ancient World: The Ancient Greeks
by Allison Lassieur (Children's Press, 2005)

Web Sites

Due to the changing nature of Internet links, PowerKids Press has developed an online list of Web sites related to the subject of this book. This site is updated regularly. Please use this link to access this list:
www.powerkidslinks.com/flash/greeks

INDEX